Title:

"Harmony of Wealth: Financial Breakthroughs through Pendulum Therapy"

Introduction:

In the fast-paced world of finance, achieving a breakthrough can often feel like navigating through uncharted waters. However, "Harmony of Wealth" introduces a revolutionary approach to financial success — Pendulum Therapy. This book delves into the intricacies of this powerful technique, offering readers a comprehensive guide to unlocking their financial potential.

In the dynamic and ever-evolving landscape of finance, individuals often find themselves grappling with the challenges of uncertainty and complexity. Navigating the currents of financial markets, investment decisions, and economic fluctuations can indeed resemble a journey through uncharted waters, where the path to breakthroughs seems elusive. In recognition of these challenges, "Harmony of Wealth" emerges as a guiding beacon, introducing a revolutionary approach to financial success: Pendulum Therapy.

This ground-breaking methodology represents a fusion of ancient wisdom and modern understanding, positioning itself as a transformative tool for those seeking not only monetary prosperity but a holistic and balanced approach to wealth. "Harmony of Wealth" serves as an entry point into the realm of Pendulum Therapy, a practice that goes beyond conventional financial advice by tapping into the realms of energy, intuition, and the subconscious mind.

As the pages unfold, the book embarks on a journey into the intricacies of Pendulum Therapy, unravelling its profound connection to the energies that underlie financial decisions. The pendulum, an ancient divination tool, becomes more than a mere instrument; it transforms into a conduit for unlocking the potential within each reader. Through the exploration of Pendulum Therapy, the book provides not only a theoretical foundation but also practical applications that empower individuals to make informed and intuitive financial choices.

The comprehensive guide within "Harmony of Wealth" is designed to meet readers where they are on their financial journey. Whether facing challenges, seeking clarity on decisions, or aiming to manifest abundance, the book offers a roadmap for personal and financial transformation. It doesn't merely scratch the surface but delves deeply into the nuanced layers of Pendulum Therapy, illustrating how this technique can serve as a catalyst for breakthroughs that extend far beyond monetary gains.

The holistic approach taken in "Harmony of Wealth" underscores the interconnectedness of one's financial life with broader aspects of well-being. The book recognizes that achieving financial success involves not only strategic planning but also an alignment of energies, a release of limiting beliefs, and the cultivation of a mindset that invites abundance. In doing so, it presents a vision of wealth that extends beyond the confines of traditional financial literature, inviting readers to embark on a journey of self-discovery and empowerment.

In essence, "Harmony of Wealth" aims to bridge the gap between the conventional and the unconventional, offering a fresh perspective on financial breakthroughs. By embracing Pendulum Therapy as a tool for navigating the complexities of the financial world, readers are invited to transcend the limitations of conventional financial advice and tap into the timeless wisdom that lies within. The book stands as an invitation to explore, question, and ultimately redefine the relationship between individuals and their financial destinies.

The Pendulum's Wisdom

Begin by exploring the origins and philosophy behind Pendulum Therapy. Understand how this ancient divination tool, used for centuries, can be harnessed to gain insights into financial decisions. Learn about the energy connection between the pendulum and the subconscious mind, setting the stage for the transformative journey ahead.

"The Pendulum's Wisdom" unfolds as a captivating exploration into the profound insights and transformative power that Pendulum Therapy holds. This ancient divination tool becomes not just a swinging weight but a conduit to the deeper recesses of the subconscious mind, offering profound wisdom that transcends the material and taps into the realms of intuition and energy.

The Dance of Energy

The journey begins by unravelling the mystical dance of energy between the pendulum and the individual. The chapter elucidates how the pendulum becomes a channel for the energies that reside within and around us. It serves as a subtle communicator, translating the vibrations of the subconscious into tangible movements that guide individuals on their path to self-discovery and, ultimately, financial wisdom.

Unlocking Subconscious Insights

Delving into the intricacies of Pendulum Therapy, this chapter demystifies the process of unlocking subconscious insights. The pendulum becomes a key that opens the door to hidden beliefs, fears, and desires related to wealth. Readers are guided through exercises that reveal the wisdom embedded in the depths of the mind, providing a clearer understanding of one's relationship with abundance.

The Language of Movement

As the pendulum swings and sways, this chapter explores the language it communicates. It becomes a unique dialect, conveying responses through distinct movements. Readers gain insight into interpreting the pendulum's language, transforming seemingly random motions into a dialogue that imparts profound wisdom. The pendulum becomes a trusted companion, whispering truths that guide financial decisions.

Pathways to Financial Clarity

Building on the foundations, this chapter delves into the specific pathways to financial clarity paved by the pendulum. Practical applications are explored, from posing targeted questions about investments to seeking guidance on budgeting strategies. The pendulum becomes a compass, directing individuals toward financial decisions aligned with their highest good.

Harmonizing Intuition and Practicality

The pendulum's wisdom extends beyond the realm of the mystical; it intertwines with practical decision-making. This chapter elucidates how Pendulum Therapy harmonizes intuition and practicality in financial choices. Readers learn to navigate the fine balance between gut feelings and informed decisions, allowing the pendulum's wisdom to guide them in achieving financial goals with a holistic approach.

Transcending Limiting Beliefs

In a transformative turn, the pendulum's wisdom is revealed as a catalyst for transcending limiting beliefs. This chapter provides a roadmap for identifying and releasing mental blocks that hinder financial abundance. The pendulum becomes a liberator, empowering individuals to rewrite their financial narratives and embrace a mindset that attracts prosperity.

The Pendulum's Gaze into the Future

The penultimate chapter explores the pendulum's

prophetic potential. It becomes
a seer, offering glimpses into
the future financial landscape.
Readers are guided through
exercises that leverage the
pendulum's wisdom for
strategic planning, helping
them anticipate and navigate
the twists and turns on their
journey to financial success.

A Symphony of Prosperity

The concluding chapter
harmonizes the various threads
of wisdom woven throughout
the book. The pendulum
emerges not merely as a tool
but as a conductor

orchestrating a symphony of prosperity. Its wisdom, harnessed through Pendulum Therapy, becomes a guiding melody that resonates with the individual, offering a transformative path toward financial abundance.

In "The Pendulum's Wisdom," readers are invited to dance with the energies, interpret the language of movement, and embrace the profound insights that emanate from the pendulum. The book serves as a guide, unlocking the rich tapestry of wisdom within, leading individuals toward financial clarity, abundance, and a deeper connection with their truest selves.

Aligning Energies for Prosperity

Discover the art of aligning personal energies with financial goals through Pendulum Therapy. Explore practical exercises to attune the mind to abundance, paving the way for a harmonious relationship with wealth. This chapter outlines a step-by-step process to create an energetic foundation for financial breakthroughs.

"Aligning Energies for Prosperity" serves as the

foundational cornerstone in the transformative journey of Pendulum Therapy toward financial abundance. This opening chapter lays the groundwork for readers, introducing them to the essential concept of energy alignment and its pivotal role in attracting prosperity.

Understanding the Energetic Blueprint

The chapter begins by elucidating the idea that every individual possesses a unique energetic blueprint that influences their financial reality. Readers are guided to explore

the interconnectedness
between personal energies and
the manifestation of wealth.
The pendulum is introduced as
a tool capable of tapping into
and harmonizing with these
energies.

Attuning the Mind to Abundance

Practical exercises are
presented to help individuals
attune their minds to the
frequency of abundance.
Through focused intention and
mindful practices, readers learn
to align their thoughts and
emotions with prosperity,
creating a fertile ground for

financial growth. The pendulum becomes a guide, indicating the degree of alignment and providing insights into areas that may require further attention.

Clearing Energetic Blockages

The chapter explores the concept of energetic blockages that can hinder the flow of abundance. Readers are introduced to Pendulum Therapy techniques designed to identify and release these blockages. The pendulum's movements serve as a diagnostic tool, revealing areas where energy may be stagnant or obstructed, paving the way for a more fluid and harmonious financial flow.

Setting Positive Intentions

Guided by the pendulum's wisdom, individuals are encouraged to set positive intentions for financial prosperity. This involves creating affirmations and declarations that resonate with the desired outcome. The chapter provides insights into how the pendulum can be used to amplify the power of positive intentions, acting as a catalyst for the manifestation of abundance.

Building a Strong Energetic Foundation

Practical steps are outlined to help readers build a strong energetic foundation for financial success. The pendulum's guidance is instrumental in determining the effectiveness of various practices, such as visualization, gratitude, and mindfulness, in fortifying this foundation. As individuals strengthen their energetic base, they are better equipped to navigate the complexities of the financial landscape.

Embracing the Law of Attraction

The chapter concludes by introducing the Law of Attraction as a guiding principle in aligning energies for prosperity. Through Pendulum Therapy, readers learn how to harness this universal law to draw positive financial experiences into their lives. The pendulum becomes a conduit for understanding the intricacies of the Law of Attraction and applying its principles to attract wealth.

In "Aligning Energies for Prosperity," readers embark on a journey of self-discovery, understanding how their energies shape their financial reality. The pendulum, as a wise companion, guides individuals in aligning their thoughts, intentions, and actions with the abundant energy of the universe. This chapter lays the groundwork for the transformative Pendulum Therapy practices that follow, setting the stage for readers to unlock their full financial potential.

Pendulum Techniques for Financial Clarity

Delve into specific Pendulum Therapy techniques designed to provide clarity on financial matters. From budgeting to investment decisions, learn how to pose precise questions to the pendulum and interpret its responses. This chapter acts as a practical guide, offering real-world applications for achieving financial insight.

"Pendulum Techniques for Financial Clarity" delves into the

practical applications of Pendulum Therapy, offering readers a comprehensive guide to gaining clear insights into various financial aspects. This chapter provides a hands-on approach, empowering individuals to pose precise questions and interpret the pendulum's responses for informed decision-making.

Formulating Targeted Questions

The chapter begins by emphasizing the importance of formulating targeted questions to extract specific information from the pendulum. Readers are guided through the art of crafting clear and unambiguous queries related to financial matters, ensuring that the responses received are insightful and actionable.

Interpreting Pendulum Movements

Practical demonstrations illustrate the various movements of the pendulum and their corresponding meanings. Whether it's the classic back-and-forth swing, circular rotations, or diagonal patterns, readers gain a nuanced understanding of how to interpret these movements in the context of financial decision-making. The pendulum becomes a symbolic language, conveying messages from the subconscious mind.

Gaining Insights into Investment Decisions

The chapter provides specific Pendulum Therapy techniques tailored to gaining clarity on investment decisions. Readers learn how to pose questions about potential investments, risk assessments, and expected returns. The pendulum becomes a valuable tool in assessing the viability and alignment of investment opportunities with individual financial goals.

Navigating Budgeting and Financial Planning

Practical exercises guide readers in using the pendulum to gain insights into budgeting and financial planning. Whether determining the most effective budget allocation or seeking guidance on long-term financial strategies, the pendulum serves as a compass, helping individuals make decisions aligned with their financial objectives.

Exploring Career and Income Opportunities

Readers are introduced to Pendulum Therapy techniques designed to explore career and income opportunities. The pendulum becomes a guide in assessing potential career paths, evaluating job opportunities, and gauging the financial implications of various professional decisions. This section empowers individuals to make choices that align with both their passion and financial goals.

Evaluating Debt Management Strategies

The chapter provides insights into using Pendulum Therapy for evaluating debt management strategies. Readers learn how to pose questions about prioritizing debt repayment, negotiating terms, and finding the most effective methods for financial relief. The pendulum becomes a tool for creating a structured and personalized approach to managing financial obligations.

Setting and Refining Financial Goals

Practical exercises guide individuals in using the pendulum to set and refine financial goals. Whether determining the feasibility of specific targets or seeking guidance on adjusting goals to align with changing circumstances, the pendulum serves as a dynamic tool for continuous goal refinement and manifestation.

Fostering Intuition in Financial Decision-Making

The chapter concludes by exploring how Pendulum Therapy can be employed to foster intuition in financial decision-making. Readers gain insights into tapping into their inner wisdom to make sound financial choices. The pendulum becomes a bridge between the rational and intuitive mind, facilitating a holistic approach to decision-making.

In "Pendulum Techniques for Financial Clarity," readers embark on a practical journey, applying Pendulum Therapy to gain actionable insights into their financial landscape. The chapter equips individuals with

the skills to use the pendulum
as a versatile tool, providing
clarity on investments,
budgeting, career decisions,
and more. It stands as a guide
for harnessing the
transformative potential of
Pendulum Therapy in the
pursuit of financial wisdom and
clarity.

Breaking Through Limiting Beliefs

Uncover the role of limiting
beliefs in hindering financial
success. Explore Pendulum
Therapy exercises aimed at
identifying and releasing these

beliefs, creating space for a mindset conducive to wealth creation. This chapter provides a roadmap for overcoming mental barriers and embracing a mindset of abundance.

Breaking Through Limiting Beliefs" is a pivotal chapter in the journey of Pendulum Therapy, guiding readers to identify, challenge, and transcend the mental barriers that hinder financial abundance. This chapter serves as a transformative catalyst, empowering individuals to reshape their beliefs and foster a mindset conducive to prosperity.

Identifying Limiting Beliefs

The chapter begins by helping readers identify limiting beliefs that may be ingrained in their subconscious minds. Practical exercises guide individuals in reflecting on their thoughts and perceptions related to money, success, and abundance. The pendulum becomes a sensitive instrument, unveiling the often-hidden beliefs that shape financial realities.

Releasing Energetic Blockages

Readers are introduced to
Pendulum Therapy techniques
aimed at releasing energetic
blockages associated with
limiting beliefs. The pendulum
becomes a tool for identifying
areas where energy may be
stagnating due to negative
thought patterns. Practical
exercises guide individuals in
using the pendulum to release
these blockages, creating space
for a more positive and
abundant mindset.

Affirmations for Financial Empowerment

The chapter provides guidance
on creating and using

affirmations to counteract
limiting beliefs. Readers learn
how to formulate positive and
empowering statements that
align with their financial goals.
The pendulum serves as a
validator, helping individuals
determine the effectiveness of
their affirmations and ensuring
they resonate with the desired
energetic frequencies.

Rewriting the Financial Narrative

Practical exercises empower
individuals to rewrite their
financial narratives. Using the
pendulum as a guide, readers
explore alternative perspectives

and stories that challenge and replace limiting beliefs. This process fosters a shift in mindset, allowing individuals to envision a financial reality unencumbered by self-imposed constraints.

Cultivating a Positive Money Mindset

The chapter emphasizes cultivating a positive money mindset through Pendulum Therapy. Readers are guided in using the pendulum to reinforce positive beliefs about money, abundance, and their own deservingness of financial success. The pendulum

becomes a tool for shaping a
mindset that attracts prosperity
and opportunities.

Addressing Fear and Resistance

Pendulum Therapy is applied to
address fear and resistance
associated with financial
growth. Readers explore the
root causes of fear and
resistance through targeted
questions posed to the
pendulum. Practical exercises
guide individuals in using the
pendulum's wisdom to develop
strategies for overcoming these
emotional barriers and
embracing financial abundance.

Integrating Pendulum Guidance into Daily Practices

The chapter concludes by offering insights into integrating Pendulum Therapy into daily practices. Readers are encouraged to incorporate pendulum-based rituals and affirmations into their routines, fostering a continuous process of breaking through limiting beliefs. The pendulum becomes a constant companion, guiding individuals toward a sustained and positive transformation of their financial mindset.

In "Breaking Through Limiting Beliefs," readers embark on a liberating journey, using Pendulum Therapy as a tool to dismantle the mental barriers that impede financial success. The chapter stands as a testament to the power of self-awareness and intention, demonstrating how the pendulum becomes a conduit for personal empowerment and a guide toward a mindset of abundance.

Mapping Your Financial Future

Navigate the path to financial breakthrough by creating a personalized roadmap. Utilize Pendulum Therapy to set clear financial goals, develop strategic plans, and make informed decisions. This chapter offers a blueprint for readers to carve out their unique journey toward financial prosperity.

"Mapping Your Financial Future" marks a crucial phase in the Pendulum Therapy journey, guiding readers to chart a course toward their desired financial destinies. This chapter serves as a strategic planner, utilizing Pendulum Therapy techniques to help individuals set clear goals, make informed decisions, and navigate the dynamic landscape of their financial futures.

Clarifying Long-Term Financial Goals

The chapter begins by guiding readers through Pendulum Therapy exercises to clarify their long-term financial goals. By posing targeted questions, individuals use the pendulum to gain insights into aspirations such as homeownership, retirement, or entrepreneurial endeavors. The pendulum becomes a compass, pointing

the way toward a vision of
financial success.

Aligning Short-Term Actions with Long-Term Objectives

Practical exercises empower individuals to align their short-term actions with long-term financial objectives. Through Pendulum Therapy, readers gain clarity on the immediate steps required to bring them closer to their overarching goals. The pendulum serves as a guide in crafting actionable plans that contribute to the realization of long-term financial aspirations.

Evaluating and Refining Financial Strategies

Readers learn how to use the pendulum to evaluate and refine their financial strategies. Whether it involves investment decisions, debt management, or income-generating activities, Pendulum Therapy becomes a tool for assessing the alignment of strategies with individual goals. The pendulum aids in refining approaches for maximum effectiveness.

Anticipating and Navigating Financial Challenges

Pendulum Therapy techniques are applied to anticipate and navigate potential financial challenges. By posing questions related to potential obstacles and developing contingency plans, individuals use the pendulum to enhance their preparedness. It becomes a strategic advisor, providing insights into overcoming hurdles on the path to financial success.

Balancing Risk and Reward

Practical exercises guide readers in using Pendulum Therapy to strike a balance between risk and reward. Whether assessing investment opportunities or considering career changes, the pendulum becomes a tool for evaluating the potential outcomes of various decisions. Readers gain insights into making calculated choices that align with their risk tolerance and financial goals.

Setting Milestones and Celebrating Achievements

The chapter encourages individuals to set milestones on their financial journey. Through Pendulum Therapy, readers gain insights into defining achievable milestones and celebrating their financial achievements along the way. The pendulum becomes a source of motivation, providing guidance on acknowledging and appreciating progress.

Adjusting Financial Plans to Life Changes

Readers explore how Pendulum Therapy can be employed to adjust financial plans in response to life changes. By posing questions related to shifts in personal circumstances, individuals use the pendulum to adapt their financial strategies accordingly.

The pendulum becomes a flexible guide, offering insights into navigating the evolving landscape of life and finances.

Integrating Intuition into Financial Decision-Making

The chapter concludes by reinforcing the integration of intuition into financial decision-making. Readers are encouraged to trust their inner guidance, cultivated through Pendulum Therapy, when making choices about their financial futures. The pendulum becomes a trusted advisor, aligning individuals with their intuition for empowered decision-making.

In "Mapping Your Financial Future," readers embark on a purposeful journey of strategic planning and empowered decision-making. By utilizing Pendulum Therapy techniques, the chapter enables individuals to shape a financial roadmap that aligns with their goals, values, and aspirations. The pendulum serves as a versatile tool, offering guidance at every turn as individuals map their unique paths to financial success.

Enhancing Intuition in Financial Decision-Making

Harness the power of intuition in financial decision-making through Pendulum Therapy. Learn how to tap into your inner wisdom to make sound investment choices and navigate the unpredictable financial landscape. This chapter emphasizes the synergy between intuition and financial success.

"Enhancing Intuition in Financial Decision-Making" is a

transformative chapter that invites readers to tap into their inner wisdom through Pendulum Therapy. This chapter provides practical guidance and exercises to foster a deep connection with intuition, empowering individuals to make sound and intuitive financial decisions.

Acknowledging the Role of Intuition

The chapter begins by acknowledging the valuable role of intuition in the decision-making process. Readers are guided to recognize that intuition is not a mysterious or

elusive force but a natural
aspect of human intelligence.
The pendulum becomes a tool
to uncover and amplify this
innate intuitive capacity.

Cultivating Mindful Awareness

Practical exercises encourage
individuals to cultivate mindful
awareness of their thoughts
and emotions related to
financial decisions. By using the
pendulum to pose reflective
questions, readers gain insights
into their intuitive responses.
The pendulum serves as a
mirror, reflecting the intuitive

signals that arise when contemplating financial choices.

Trusting Gut Feelings in Financial Matters

Readers explore the concept of trusting gut feelings as a valid and reliable source of guidance in financial matters. Through Pendulum Therapy, the chapter offers exercises to help individuals distinguish between rational analysis and intuitive nudges. The pendulum becomes a validator, confirming the authenticity of gut feelings as valuable indicators.

Posing Intuitive Questions to the Pendulum

The chapter introduces specific Pendulum Therapy techniques for posing intuitive questions. Readers learn how to phrase queries that invite intuitive insights, allowing the pendulum to respond to the deeper wisdom within. The pendulum becomes a conduit for intuition, providing nuanced guidance on financial decisions.

Integrating Intuition with Analytical Thinking

Practical exercises guide
readers in integrating intuition
with analytical thinking. By
combining rational analysis with
intuitive insights gained
through Pendulum Therapy,
individuals develop a holistic
approach to financial decision-
making. The pendulum
becomes a bridge between the
conscious and subconscious,
facilitating a balanced and
informed decision-making
process.

Recognizing Subtle Signs and Synchronicities

The chapter explores the recognition of subtle signs and synchronicities as intuitive messages. Readers learn to observe and interpret the symbolic language of the universe, seeking guidance through Pendulum Therapy. The pendulum becomes a divining rod, helping individuals discern meaningful patterns and align with the flow of intuitive guidance.

Embracing Intuitive Action Steps

Readers are encouraged to embrace intuitive action steps in their financial journeys. Through Pendulum Therapy, individuals gain insights into the specific actions that align with their intuitive guidance. The pendulum becomes a compass, directing individuals toward choices that resonate with their inner knowing.

Trusting the Timing of Financial Decisions

Practical exercises guide individuals in trusting the timing of their financial decisions. By using the pendulum to explore the most opportune moments for action, readers learn to synchronize their actions with the natural flow of energy. The pendulum becomes a timekeeper, guiding individuals to trust the unfolding of their financial paths.

Cultivating a Lifestyle of Intuitive Financial Wisdom

The chapter concludes by encouraging individuals to cultivate a lifestyle of intuitive financial wisdom. By consistently practicing Pendulum Therapy and embracing intuitive decision-making, readers develop a heightened awareness of their financial choices. The pendulum becomes an ongoing ally, supporting individuals in navigating the complexities of their financial landscapes with intuition as a guiding light.

In "Enhancing Intuition in Financial Decision-Making," readers embark on a journey of self-discovery, learning to trust their inner guidance in financial matters. The chapter underscores the symbiotic relationship between Pendulum Therapy and intuition, offering a holistic approach to decision-making that honors both rational analysis and intuitive wisdom. The pendulum becomes a trusted companion, guiding individuals to align with their intuitive knowing on their path to financial empowerment.

Manifesting Abundance

Explore advanced Pendulum Therapy techniques to manifest abundance in your financial life. From visualization exercises to energy alignment rituals, discover ways to amplify the power of the pendulum in attracting wealth. This chapter serves as a guide to incorporating manifestation practices into your daily routine.

"Manifesting Abundance" is a chapter that serves as a powerful guide, utilizing Pendulum Therapy to help readers harness the energy of manifestation for creating abundance in their financial and personal lives. This transformative chapter provides practical exercises and insights to align thoughts, intentions, and actions with the vibration of prosperity.

Understanding the Law of Attraction

The chapter begins by introducing readers to the foundational principles of the Law of Attraction. Through Pendulum Therapy, individuals explore how their thoughts and energies contribute to the manifestation process. The pendulum becomes a tool for understanding the connection between energy, intention, and the attraction of abundance.

Clarifying Abundance Intentions

Practical exercises guide individuals in using the pendulum to clarify their intentions for abundance. Readers explore specific areas of their financial and personal lives where they seek prosperity. The pendulum becomes a precise instrument, helping individuals articulate their desires and align their energies with the manifestation of abundance.

Affirming Positive Abundance Statements

Readers are encouraged to create positive abundance statements aligned with their

intentions. Through Pendulum
Therapy, individuals learn to
formulate affirmations that
resonate with the energy of
prosperity. The pendulum
serves as a validator, confirming
the potency of these positive
statements and assisting in
their integration into daily
thoughts and affirmations.

Visualizing Abundance
with the Pendulum

Practical exercises involve using
the pendulum to enhance
visualization techniques for
manifesting abundance.
Readers learn how to create
vivid mental images of their

desired financial and personal scenarios. The pendulum becomes a guide, amplifying the power of visualization to influence the subconscious mind and attract abundance.

Aligning Actions with Manifestation Goals

The chapter guides individuals in using Pendulum Therapy to align their daily actions with their manifestation goals. Readers explore how to pose questions to the pendulum about specific actions that support the attraction of abundance. The pendulum becomes a compass, providing

guidance on steps that resonate
with the manifested reality they
seek.

Releasing Resistance to Abundance

Practical exercises involve using
Pendulum Therapy to identify
and release resistance to
abundance. Readers explore
questions related to any
underlying fears or doubts that
may hinder the manifestation
process. The pendulum
becomes a tool for clearing

energetic blockages, allowing individuals to create a more open and receptive space for abundance.

Leveraging Gratitude for Manifestation

Readers learn how to leverage the power of gratitude in the manifestation process. Through Pendulum Therapy, individuals explore questions related to gratitude practices and their impact on abundance. The pendulum becomes a teacher, guiding individuals to cultivate a mindset of gratitude that enhances the manifestation of prosperity.

Setting a Manifestation Ritual with the Pendulum

The chapter concludes by guiding individuals in setting up a manifestation ritual using the pendulum. Readers explore personalized rituals that incorporate Pendulum Therapy techniques. The pendulum becomes a sacred tool, enhancing the energy of the ritual and amplifying the intentions for manifesting abundance.

Nurturing Patience and Trust

Throughout the chapter, individuals are encouraged to nurture patience and trust in the manifestation process. Pendulum Therapy serves as a constant companion, providing reassurance and insights when faced with challenges or delays. The pendulum becomes a symbol of unwavering trust in the unfolding journey toward abundance.

In "Manifesting Abundance," readers embark on a journey of intentional creation, using Pendulum Therapy as a catalyst for aligning with the energies of prosperity. The chapter empowers individuals to

actively participate in the
manifestation process,
leveraging the wisdom of the
pendulum to create a life rich in
financial and personal
abundance.

Navigating Economic Challenges

Address economic challenges
with resilience and adaptability
using Pendulum Therapy.
Understand how to interpret
the pendulum's guidance
during times of financial
uncertainty, enabling you to

make strategic decisions that weather the storms. This chapter provides insights into maintaining financial equilibrium in the face of external pressures.

"Navigating Economic Challenges" is a timely and practical chapter that equips readers with Pendulum Therapy techniques to navigate uncertainties, downturns, and economic challenges. By integrating Pendulum Therapy into their financial decision-making process, individuals gain insights and guidance on how to adapt and thrive despite economic fluctuations.

Assessing Economic Trends

The chapter begins by guiding readers to use Pendulum Therapy to assess current economic trends. Through targeted questions, individuals gain insights into potential economic shifts and how these trends may impact their financial circumstances. The pendulum becomes a reliable guide, providing nuanced perspectives on navigating economic uncertainties.

Evaluating Financial Resilience

Practical exercises involve using the pendulum to evaluate one's financial resilience in the face of economic challenges. Readers explore questions related to their financial stability, emergency preparedness, and adaptability. The pendulum becomes a diagnostic tool, helping individuals identify areas of strength and areas that may need attention.

Making Informed Investment Decisions

Pendulum Therapy is applied to guide individuals in making informed investment decisions during economic challenges.

Readers pose questions to the pendulum about potential investment opportunities, risk management, and the alignment of investments with their financial goals. The pendulum becomes a strategic advisor, offering insights into navigating the complexities of the financial markets.

Creating a Contingency Plan

Practical exercises guide individuals in using Pendulum Therapy to create a contingency plan for economic challenges. Readers explore questions related to potential scenarios and develop action steps to mitigate financial risks. The pendulum becomes a planning tool, assisting individuals in preparing for unexpected economic events.

Adapting Career Strategies

The chapter provides insights into using Pendulum Therapy to adapt career strategies during economic challenges. Readers explore questions about career shifts, skill development, and potential opportunities. The pendulum becomes a career advisor, offering guidance on aligning professional paths with economic trends.

Identifying Alternative Income Streams

Practical exercises involve using the pendulum to identify alternative income streams during economic challenges. Readers explore questions related to diversifying income sources, exploring side hustles, and adapting to changing market demands. The pendulum becomes a visionary guide, assisting individuals in identifying creative ways to supplement their income.

Managing Debt Effectively

Readers learn how to use Pendulum Therapy to manage debt effectively during economic challenges. Through targeted questions, individuals gain insights into debt repayment strategies, negotiating terms, and alleviating financial burdens. The pendulum becomes a debt management advisor, offering guidance on navigating debt-related challenges.

Cultivating a Resilient Mindset

The chapter emphasizes the importance of cultivating a resilient mindset through Pendulum Therapy. Readers explore questions related to mindset shifts, adapting to change, and maintaining a positive outlook during economic challenges. The pendulum becomes a mindset coach, providing insights into fostering resilience and a proactive approach to challenges.

Planning for Long-Term Financial Stability

The chapter concludes by guiding individuals to use

Pendulum Therapy for planning long-term financial stability. Readers explore questions related to future financial goals, retirement planning, and creating a sustainable financial roadmap. The pendulum becomes a visionary guide, offering insights into building a foundation for enduring financial well-being.

In "Navigating Economic Challenges," readers leverage the wisdom of Pendulum Therapy to navigate the complexities of economic uncertainties. The chapter empowers individuals to make informed decisions, adapt to changing circumstances, and proactively plan for a resilient financial future. The pendulum becomes an invaluable tool, offering clarity and guidance in the midst of economic challenges.

"Harmony of Wealth" concludes with a reminder of the transformative potential inherent in Pendulum Therapy. Empowered with the wisdom of this ancient practice, readers are equipped to navigate the complexities of the financial world and achieve lasting breakthroughs. The book serves as a beacon, guiding individuals towards a harmonious relationship with wealth and a future filled with financial abundance.

Epilogue: Sustaining Financial Harmony

As we reach the end of our journey together, it's essential to acknowledge that financial breakthroughs are not merely one-time events but ongoing processes. The principles of Pendulum Therapy introduced in this book are timeless tools that can be integrated into your daily life to maintain financial harmony.

Reflect on the transformative experiences shared within these pages and consider how Pendulum Therapy has become an integral part of your financial decision-making. The epilogue offers insights into building a sustainable financial future by consistently applying the principles learned throughout the book.

When using a pendulum for financial abundance, it's important to approach it with a clear and positive mindset. The following are example commands or questions you can ask the pendulum to help align your energies with

financial abundance.
Remember to phrase your
questions in a way that allows
for a clear "yes" or "no"
response from the pendulum.

Setting the Intention:

"Pendulum, I am open to
receiving guidance for financial
abundance. May the energies
align positively to attract
prosperity into my life. Show
me a 'yes' response for
affirmation."

Clarity on Financial Decisions:

"Pendulum, should I proceed
with [specific financial decision]
for my highest good and
financial abundance?"

"Is the path I am considering for
wealth creation in alignment
with my true purpose?"

Overcoming Limiting Beliefs:

"Pendulum, am I holding onto
any limiting beliefs that are
obstructing my financial
abundance?"

"Can you guide me in releasing
any subconscious blocks
preventing financial success?"

Financial Goal-Setting:

"Pendulum, is my current financial goal of [specific amount or objective] realistic and achievable?"

"Can you provide guidance on the steps I need to take to manifest my financial goals?"

Investment Decisions:

"Pendulum, is [specific investment] a wise choice for me to pursue financial growth?"

"Should I diversify my investments for greater financial stability?"

Energy Alignment for Manifestation:

"Pendulum, can you guide me in aligning my energy with the frequency of financial abundance?"

"Is there a specific practice or ritual that will enhance the manifestation of financial prosperity in my life?"

Timing and Patience:

"Pendulum, can you provide insight into the timing of when my financial abundance will manifest?"

"Is there a lesson or aspect of patience that I need to embrace on my financial journey?"

Staying Resilient in Challenges:

"Pendulum, will I overcome the current financial challenges I am facing?"

"Can you offer guidance on maintaining resilience and optimism during economic uncertainties?"

Remember to use these commands as a starting point and adapt them to your specific situation. The key is to maintain a positive and open mindset while using the pendulum as a tool for guidance on your financial journey.

Affirmations and Declarations:

"Pendulum, can you assist me in creating powerful affirmations that resonate with financial abundance?"

"Is there a specific affirmation I should focus on daily to attract wealth into my life?"

Balancing Work and Wealth:

"Pendulum, should I explore new opportunities for career

advancement to enhance my financial situation?"

"Can you guide me in achieving a harmonious balance between work and wealth creation?"

Opportunities for Growth:

"Pendulum, are there unseen opportunities for financial growth that I should be aware of?"

"Can you provide insight into avenues I may not have considered for expanding my financial abundance?"

Gratitude and Appreciation:

"Pendulum, is expressing gratitude an important aspect of attracting financial abundance into my life?"

"Can you guide me in cultivating a mindset of appreciation for the wealth I already have?"

Networking and Collaborations:

"Pendulum, should I seek out new connections or collaborations to enhance my financial prospects?"

"Is there a specific network or group that would be beneficial for my financial growth?"

Debt Management:

"Pendulum, can you provide guidance on the most effective strategy for managing and reducing my debt?"

"Should I focus on paying off specific debts first for overall financial improvement?"

Continual Self-Reflection:

"Pendulum, is regular self-reflection important for

maintaining a clear financial
vision?"

"Can you guide me in
understanding any personal
habits or behaviours that may
be influencing my financial
situation?"

Celebrating Financial Milestones:

"Pendulum, is it beneficial for
me to celebrate small financial
achievements along my
journey?"

"Can you suggest a meaningful
way for me to acknowledge and
appreciate my financial
milestones?"

Remember to trust your intuition and use the pendulum as a tool to gain insights, but always complement it with practical actions. The combination of intention, positive energy, and informed decision-making can contribute to your financial abundance and success.

Evaluating Financial Opportunities:

"Pendulum, can you assist me in evaluating the potential risks and benefits of the current financial opportunity before me?"

"Is there additional information
or due diligence I should
consider before making a
financial decision?"

Cultivating a Wealth Mindset:

"Pendulum, can you guide me
in adopting a mindset that
attracts wealth effortlessly?"

"Is there a specific mindset shift
I need to make to align with my
financial goals?"

Integrating Financial Wisdom:

"Pendulum, is there ancient or
timeless financial wisdom that I

should incorporate into my approach?"

"Can you provide insights into financial principles that have stood the test of time?"

Balancing Giving and Receiving:

"Pendulum, is there a balance between giving and receiving that I should strive for in my financial journey?"

"Can you guide me in finding ways to give back and contribute to others as part of my wealth-building path?"

Financial Education and Growth:

"Pendulum, should I invest time and resources in furthering my financial education?"

"Can you provide guidance on specific areas of financial knowledge I should focus on for personal and professional growth?"

Visualizing Financial Success:

"Pendulum, is regular visualization of my financial goals an effective practice for manifestation?"

"Can you guide me in creating a vivid mental image of the financial success I aim to achieve?"

Building Resilience to Market Changes:

"Pendulum, can you assist me in developing resilience to navigate market fluctuations and economic changes?"

"Is there a mindset or strategy that will help me adapt to unforeseen financial challenges?"

Aligning Actions with Financial Goals:

"Pendulum, are my current
daily actions in alignment with
my long-term financial goals?"

"Can you guide me in making
adjustments to my daily routine
to better support my financial
aspirations?"

Embracing Abundance in All Areas:

"Pendulum, can you help me
expand my definition of
abundance beyond finances to
encompass overall well-being?"

"Is there a holistic approach to abundance that I should incorporate into my life?"

In your journey toward financial abundance with Pendulum Therapy, adapt and personalize these commands to suit your unique circumstances. Remember that the pendulum serves as a tool for self-discovery and guidance, but taking proactive steps and staying open to opportunities are crucial aspects of your financial breakthrough. May your path be filled with prosperity, wisdom, and the continuous realization of your financial goals.

Affirming Financial Independence:

"Pendulum, can you guide me in affirming my financial independence and autonomy?"

"Is there a specific affirmation that empowers me to take control of my financial destiny?"

Exploring Alternative Income Streams:

"Pendulum, should I explore alternative sources of income to diversify and enhance my financial stability?"

"Can you provide insights into potential avenues for creating additional streams of wealth?"

Optimizing Financial Decisions:

"Pendulum, can you assist me in optimizing my financial decisions for the highest good?"

"Is there a specific strategy or approach that will lead to more favourable outcomes in my financial endeavours?"

Maintaining Financial Discipline:

"Pendulum, can you guide me
in maintaining discipline in my
financial habits and routines?"

"Is there a daily practice that
will support my commitment to
financial discipline?"

Harnessing Positive Financial Energy:

"Pendulum, can you assist me
in harnessing positive energy
for financial abundance?"

"Is there a ritual or practice that
will help me cultivate and
sustain positive financial
vibrations?"

Attracting Prosperous Relationships:

"Pendulum, can you provide insights into attracting relationships that support my financial growth?"

"Is there a specific energy I should cultivate to align with individuals who contribute positively to my financial journey?"

Checking Financial Alignment Regularly:

"Pendulum, is it beneficial for me to regularly check the alignment of my financial goals

with my current life
circumstances?"

"Can you guide me in adapting
my financial goals to align with
my evolving life path?"

Fostering Gratitude for Financial Lessons:

"Pendulum, can you help me
cultivate gratitude for the
financial lessons, whether
positive or challenging?"

"Is there a mindset shift that
will allow me to appreciate the
growth opportunities within
financial experiences?"

Empowering Financial Visualization Techniques:

"Pendulum, can you enhance my ability to visualize and manifest my financial goals through focused intention?"

"Is there a specific visualization technique that resonates with my energy for financial success?"

Balancing Short-Term Gains with Long-Term Stability:

"Pendulum, can you guide me in striking a balance between pursuing short-term gains and maintaining long-term financial stability?"

"Is there a strategy that aligns with both immediate financial needs and enduring prosperity?"

As you incorporate these commands into your Pendulum Therapy practice, remember that the key lays not only in asking questions but also in listening to the subtle guidance that unfolds. May your journey towards financial abundance be guided by wisdom, clarity, and an unwavering belief in your own power to manifest prosperity.

Reader's Guide

Concluding the book, the
reader's guide offers
suggestions for integrating
Pendulum Therapy practices
into daily life. It encourages
readers to embark on a
continuous journey of self-
discovery, financial growth, and
personal empowerment.

In the spirit of "Harmony of
Wealth," may this book serve as
a catalyst for positive change in
your financial life. As you
navigate the dynamic landscape

of wealth creation, remember
that the power to achieve
breakthroughs lays within you.
Embrace the wisdom of the
pendulum, trust your intuition,
and may your journey toward
financial prosperity be both
fulfilling and enduring.

The end is not a destination but
a new beginning—a
continuation of the harmonious
dance between you and the
wealth you are destined to
create.

end

www.ingramcontent.com/pod-product-compliance
Lightning Source LLC
Chambersburg PA
CBHW070902260726
48661CB00004B/1553